The Wedding Shoes

The Wedding Shoes

Sufiya Ahmed

Abeeha Tariq

Collins

Contents

You're invited!

Mr Ashraf Khan and Mrs Zahra Khan request the pleasure of

............................YOU............................

to the occasion of the Nikaah ceremony and wedding reception of their beloved daughter

ANISA

to

Sajid

Son of Mr Faiz Hussain and Mrs Aaliyah Hussain

on 22nd July at the Wedding Hall.

The wedding hall

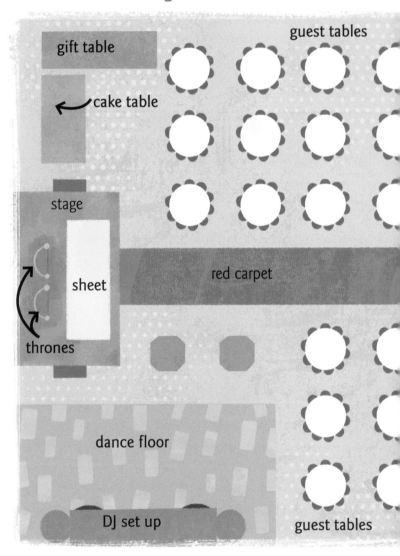

guest tables

gift table

cake table

stage

sheet

red carpet

thrones

dance floor

DJ set up

guest tables

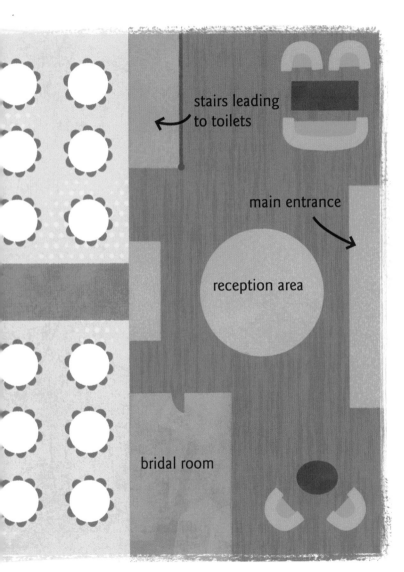

stairs leading to toilets

main entrance

reception area

bridal room

5

Meet the families

Khan family tree

Hanif —— Fatima

Ashraf —— Zahra   Zoya —— Salman

Anisa   Farah

Sana   Rehan   Ahsan

Hussain family tree

Humera ⚊ Bashir (died)

Faiz ⚊ Aaliyah   Afshan   Tahir ⚊ Millie

Sajid   Naz   Umar

Chapter 1
The wedding hall

Farah peeped her head around the door.

"It's me," she said, slipping into the bridal room in the hall where the wedding was taking place. The room looked like a train had sped through it at top speed. Every surface seemed to be scattered with make-up and hair-styling equipment.

Seema, the make-up artist, turned around, revealing the bride perched on the stool. Farah's eyes widened at the sight of her sister. Anisa looked incredible in her red wedding outfit which was made up of threads and glistening beads.

"You look beautiful," Farah marvelled.

"You think so?" Anisa asked, looking pleased.

"You look like you've stepped out of a bridal magazine," Farah gushed. "I don't think Sajid-bhai's going to recognise you. He might think someone has stolen his bride and replaced her with a fairy princess."

"Aww, that's so sweet," Anisa said.

"Just a bit of setting spray and then we're done," Seema said, spritzing the air around Anisa's face.

"Can I have a look now?" Anisa begged.

Farah's mouth fell open. Seema had arrived at 1 p.m. It was now 4 p.m. on the wedding day and she couldn't believe that Anisa hadn't peeped in the mirror in all that time. Anisa was always checking her reflection and taking selfies to build her online followers.

Anisa rose on shaky feet to turn towards the mirror. A gasp escaped her lips.

"I love it," she said breathlessly. "Thank you."

Seema was already packing her belongings.

"You're one of the most beautiful brides I've ever seen," she said, without looking up from her case.

Farah wondered if she said that to all brides who hired her.

"Oh, thank you," Anisa said, still admiring herself in the mirror.

"Now, if you could just pay me, I'll be on my way," Seema said.

Anisa pulled an envelope out of her handbag. Farah gulped as Anisa counted the £50 notes. That was more money than she had ever seen. This wedding must be costing quite a bit, with the family's outfits, the hall, the food and the decorations. However, Farah was also hoping to make some more money herself at the wedding.

And all she had to do was steal the groom's shoes.

It was a game played in many Asian weddings and Farah knew she had to win because her archenemy from school was going to play on the groom's side. The girl's name was Naz and she was the leader of a big group of girls that never included Farah in their playtime games. To get back at Naz for leaving her out, Farah ignored Naz all the time. Everyone in class knew that the two girls disliked each other.

Farah slipped out of the bridal room just as Anisa's three best friends arrived. They were going to wait with Anisa until it was time for her to enter the main wedding hall. That would be after the groom and his party had arrived. Farah stepped into the main hall which was full of loud chatter. The guests that were invited from the bride's family were already seated at the round tables and cheerfully talking to each other.

Farah's gaze fell on the main stage at the other end of the hall. It was decked in pink and white flowers, and in the centre stood two grand, throne-like chairs. They were for the bride and groom on their special day.

"*As salaam alaikum,*" said guest after guest, as Farah walked through the hall. She was busily searching for her three cousins, but she smiled and responded to the greeting which meant "peace be with you" in Arabic.

"*Walikum salaam.*"

Now where were those cousins of hers? Ah, there they were, already seated at a table. Rehan, Ahsan and Sana were six-year-old triplets who would make very good partners for Farah's mission today – and she needed all the help she could get. The groom's side would not just give up the shoes. They probably had a battle plan ready to protect them.

"Are we clear on the plan for Mission Wedding Shoes?" Farah asked, hands on hips.

The triplets nodded.

"We have to grab Sajid-bhai's shoes, no matter how hard it is," Rehan said.

"That's right," Farah said.

"I hope his feet don't smell," Sana muttered, wrinkling her nose.

"They won't!" Farah reassured her. "It's his wedding day. I'm sure he's had a good wash."

"Won't his family be guarding his shoes?" Rehan asked. "Our mum said they won't just hand them over."

"Exactly right!" Farah said. "They will try their best to hide them, but it is our job to find them and only hand them back when Sajid-bhai agrees to pay us."

Ahsan looked like he had questions, but the sound of a beating drum carried through the air before he could ask one. The triplets jumped to their feet. They loved to dance.

"They're here! They're here!" a voice called excitedly from the doors at the front of the hall.

Excitement filled the air. The groom's family had arrived, and the wedding celebrations were about to begin.

Chairs screeched on the wooden floors as a dozen aunties rose to their feet to jostle their way forward. Farah found herself being pushed aside as they hurried past.

Hoisting her skirt up above her ankles, Farah elbowed her way to the front to take prime position as the bride's only sister. Her mum was already there, clutching a garland of flowers and giggling nervously. It was her job to place them around the groom's neck to welcome him.

Chapter 2
The Nikaah

The drummer's rhythm increased and songs filled
the air. Everybody on the groom's side danced
joyously entering the wedding venue. In the middle of
them all sat the groom, high up on his white horse.
It was an impressive sight. Sajid looked like a prince
in an Indian fairytale in his gold brocade tunic and
red turban.

The aunties began to throw confetti on the guests
to welcome them to the venue.

Farah didn't throw confetti or dance like everyone else. Her eyes had found the person she was looking for. The person she would now be related to. The girl who had stopped dancing to stare back at Farah with equal dislike.

Naz – Sajid's sister.

And Farah's archenemy from school.

Today they would prove who was better, stronger and cleverer by winning the mission for the wedding shoes.

Sajid and his parents walked to the stage, removed their shoes and sat down cross-legged on the padded white sheet. They waited to be joined by Anisa and her parents. This was the most formal part of the wedding.

The rest of Sajid's family and friends took their seats at the tables and waited for the ceremony to begin.

Still standing by the hall's entrance, Farah wished Anisa would hurry up so they could start the walk down the aisle. Every passing second was an opportunity for Naz to grab her brother's shoes and hide them from the bride's family.

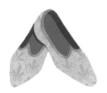

Farah thought it odd that she hadn't done so already. Perhaps it was because the shoes were visible to all the guests and Naz felt too shy to walk up and take them.

Farah craned her neck. Where was Naz sitting? Ah, there she was on Table 1.

The sound of giggling filled the reception area and Farah glanced back over her shoulder. Anisa's friends had emerged from the bridal room to go and take their seats in the hall. Farah slipped past them to stand with her mum and dad.

It was time for the bride's grand entrance.

Anisa stepped out into the foyer. Her dupatta looked very heavy as it rested on her head. It hid her face like a veil. Once their marriage ceremony is complete, Sajid will lift it and reveal Anisa's face to all the guests.

"I can't believe my little girl is getting married," Farah's dad said tearfully.

"Now's not the time to start sobbing, Dad," Anisa squeaked from under the dupatta. "You'll make me cry too."

Farah's dad dabbed his eyes with a tissue.

"Pull yourself together," Farah's mum said gently. "All the guests are waiting for the ceremony to start, we have to go."

Farah reached out and squeezed her dad's hand. "It's all right, Dad, you've still got me."

"I do, indeed," he said, giving her a small smile.

Farah picked up a bowl of pink petals from the side table and took her position in front of her family. Her mum and dad linked their arms through Anisa's, ready to lead her up the aisle.

Farah scattered the petals as she walked slowly up the strip of red carpet in the centre of the hall. The women "oohed" and "aahed" when they saw Anisa.

Farah stopped by Table 2 and sat down next to Sana as her parents continued to walk to the stage with her sister. Farah's parents slowly helped Anisa climb the steps to the stage and then they all removed their shoes. Sajid smiled widely as Anisa and her parents sat down on the padded sheet. There was now a pin-drop silence in the hall.

The marriage ceremony, the Nikaah, was about to start.

The Imam walked on and sat between Sajid and Anisa. He picked up the microphone and began the ceremony.

Farah couldn't focus on the Nikaah. All she could think about was the shoes in front of her, teasing her with their unguarded availability. Perhaps she could grab them now as everyone was focused on the Nikaah. She stood up and edged forward. Just a few more steps and she would have them.

Gosh, this was easier than she thought it would be. The groom's family obviously didn't care about protecting the shoes and, oh –

Someone pushed past Farah and sent her flying sideways into a table. The impact caused a massive centrepiece made of carved ice to wobble. It was a good thing that Aunty Shazia's henna-covered hands managed to grab the ice sculpture before it toppled over.

Farah flashed a grateful smile to her mum's best friend. Anisa had been planning her wedding day for months and pored over every detail. She would not be very happy to see her ice sculptures crashing down.

Farah straightened and glanced around. Someone had pushed her. Was it Naz? She was nowhere in sight. Farah turned towards the stage, ready to grab the shoes, and then froze when her eyes fell on the empty spot where the shoes had been only seconds ago.

She looked around wildly for the culprit and then spotted her in the corner.

Naz smirked and held up the shoes.

Round one to the groom's side.

Farah scowled. She would have to work quickly to get them back.

"*Mubarak!*"

Chants of congratulations echoed around the hall. The Nikaah was complete and Sajid and Anisa were now married. Sajid leant forward to raise Anisa's dupatta off her face. He stared at her. It was as if he couldn't believe she was his wife. They made their way slowly to their thrones and sat down as their family members gathered around them.

Naz made her way onto the stage and placed the shoes by Sajid's feet. He gave his little sister a thumbs up. She had saved his shoes, and his money.

Wedding outfits

bride

tikka

turban

groom

bangles

bridal lehenga

sherwani

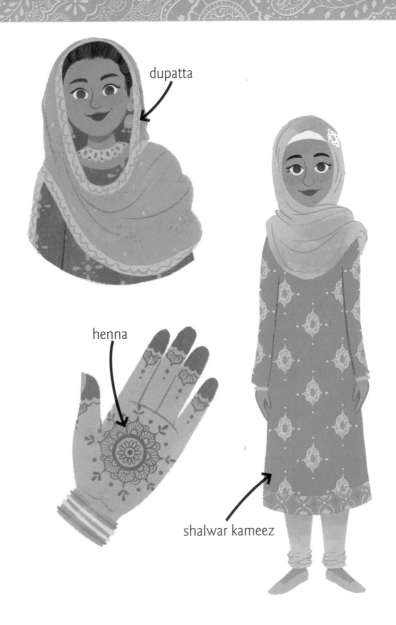

dupatta

henna

shalwar kameez

Chapter 3
The favours

Farah watched miserably from below. She couldn't believe she had lost the game so quickly. It was just embarrassing.

"Farah, look!" Sana said, coming up next to her and pointing to something on the stage.

Farah followed Sana's finger to see her cousins had sprung into action. Rehan and Ahsan slipped behind the thrones and disappeared out of sight. Then two pairs of little hands crept from under Sajid's throne and grabbed a shoe each. They scrambled up and dashed to the edge of the stage before anyone from the groom's side had even noticed.

"Well done!" Farah cried, running to meet them.

She held the shoes up triumphantly in the air.

"Whoop! Whoop!" Anisa's friends who were sitting at a nearby table cheered loudly.

Rehan and Ahsan raised their fists in the air. They had won.

Up on the stage, Naz scowled and folded her arms.

Farah glanced at her enemy. She could tell that Naz was getting ready to strike back. Farah knew she would have to guard the shoes with her life. There was no way she was putting them down.

Farah's mum marched up with a large basket.

"It's time to hand out the favours," she said. "Make sure you don't miss a single guest."

Ah, the favours! Farah had forgotten all about
the sugared treats that had to be given as gifts to
celebrate the Nikaah. She and her mum had spent
the whole of last Wednesday making up the little bags
of sweets for the guests.

"Where should I hide the shoes?" Farah wailed.

Rehan tapped his chin. "Why don't you put them
at the bottom of the favours basket," he suggested.

"Great idea!" Farah said. "Come with me,
you three."

They retreated to the corner with the basket.
Rehan and Ahsan stood guard while Sana and Farah
buried the shoes deep inside the basket.

The four of them walked through the hall, handing out a favour to each guest.

"Hey girl!" an elderly lady called.

Farah turned around. "Yes?"

"I'm Aunty Humera and I need you to help me up the stairs to the ladies' loo please," she said.

Farah couldn't say "no."

"I'll be glad to help," she said.

She balanced the basket on one arm and led Aunty Humera by the other.

"You'll have to put that basket down and help me with both hands up the stairs," Aunty Humera said.

Farah hesitated and looked over her shoulder.

Where are the triplets? thought Farah. She should hand the basket to them.

"Child, let's go," said Aunty Humera.

Farah managed a small smile and placed the basket by the side of the stairs. Satisfied that it was partly hidden from view, she placed an arm around Aunty Humera and helped her with each step. When they both returned after a good ten minutes, Aunty Humera patted Farah's cheek.

"Thank you, dear," she said. "I'll make my own way to my table."

"Don't you need me to help you?" Farah asked, confused.

"I'll be fine," Aunty Humera said, walking away.

Farah stared after her. How strange that she didn't need any help now. Shrugging, she turned to the side of the stairs to pick up the basket – and froze.

The shoes were gone. The basket was empty!

Her heart began to bang in her chest. Had she just been fooled by an elderly aunty? Surely not. This was a game for the children, adults stayed out of it.

Farah hurried back into the main hall. Where was Aunty Humera? Ah, there she was and – Farah wanted to scream at the sight before her.

Aunty Humera was laughing with none other than Naz.

Farah had been tricked! Oh, how could she have fallen for it? She should never have put the basket down.

She watched furiously as a young boy went up to Naz and held out a shoe box. Naz grinned and peered in it. She gave the boy a thumbs up and then placed the shoes inside. The boy closed the lid and handed the box to Naz.

There was something else in the box with the shoes.

What was it?

Farah stormed over to them. "That was unfair," she accused Aunty Humera. "Adults aren't meant to play."

"Don't talk to my nani-ma like that!" Naz snapped.

So, Aunty Humera is Naz's grandmother, Farah thought.

"All is fair in love and war," Aunty Humera said kindly. "Now it's your turn to get the shoes back."

"I will!" Farah retorted.

Naz smirked. "Good luck."

Farah wanted to snatch the box, but she knew she couldn't. It was against the rules to take them from someone's hands.

"Who are you?" Farah asked the boy who had handed Naz the box.

"I'm Umar," he replied. "Naz is my cousin."

"There's something in the box with the shoes," Farah said. "What is it?"

"Top secret!" Umar grinned.

Music suddenly filled the hall and some of the guests headed to the dance floor.

"Let's go dance," Naz said, dragging Umar by the hand.

Farah scowled as she watched them disappear into the crowd of dancers. What should she do now? Perhaps she should find the triplets, as she needed their help. But where were they?

She soon spotted Rehan and Ahsan's heads above everyone else on the dance floor. Their dad had lifted both his sons up into his arms. Farah scowled as father and sons bobbed as one to the music. She waved her arms to catch their attention, but Rehan and Ahsan failed to notice her. They were too busy having a good time.

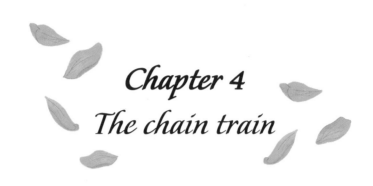

Chapter 4
The chain train

Farah left them to have fun and went in search
of Sana instead. Farah soon found her swaying
to the music all by herself. She weaved between
the dancers to reach her. Grabbing Sana's hand,
Farah raised her voice so she could be heard above
the music.

"Naz and her cousin are in the middle of the dance
floor with the shoes in a blue box. We need to get
them back."

Sana's face lit up. "The shoes are in a box!
Oh, I'm glad. I really didn't want to touch
Sajid-bhai's shoes."

Sana crouched down, looking through the gaps in the dancers' legs.

"There! They've placed the shoes on the floor and are dancing around them in a circle."

Farah dropped down next to her. "Ooh, big mistake to put the shoes down," she said.
"I should know."

"Can you see them?" Sana asked.

"I can, and well done!" Farah patted Sana's head.

Sana looked like she would burst from the praise.

"Come on," Farah urged her, edging in between the dancers. "But we have to stay hidden from view like lionesses – and then we strike."

"Roar!" Sana clawed the air with her hands.

Farah laughed. "Let's blend in."

They bobbed from side to side with the music and then suddenly, Farah found herself being grabbed by strong hands which twirled her around. It was Aunty Shazia.

Farah laughed and tried to untwine her fingers, but Aunty Shazia was in no mood to let her go and held on tight. That was until the DJ changed the tune. The crowd recognised the new beat and threw their hands in the air and sang.

Farah took advantage of her free hands and darted away from Aunty Shazia.

There was no better chance than now to grab the shoes. This song was the train chain where the dancers held on to each other's shoulder and danced around the hall.

Farah watched like a predator, ready to strike as soon as Naz joined the chain. She didn't have to wait long. Umar grabbed Naz's waist and pushed her forward so Naz had no choice but to latch onto the person in front.

Farah sprang into action. She dived forward and grabbed the shoes.

The bride's side was back in the game.

Before Farah could check what was in the box with the shoes, she was called to the stage for the family photographs.

The bride's family and all the aunts, uncles and cousins posed with the bride and groom.

Farah took centre stage as Anisa's only sister.

"Lose the box, please," the photographer called.

"Put that box aside," Farah's mum said.

"But the shoes –" There was no way Farah was going to leave the box unguarded. She and Naz had both made that mistake and paid the price! Farah glanced over her shoulder. Sana was standing by her mum on the outer circle of family members.

"I'm putting this by your feet," Farah said. "Make sure the other side don't grab it."

Sana nodded. "I'll look after it."

The photographer took his time taking the photos and Farah soon grew bored.

When all the cousins, aunts and uncles left the stage, Sajid's family came up for their photographs. Naz was made to stand beside Farah, and no matter how much the photographer cajoled them, both girls refused to remove the scowls off their faces. They could barely stand to look at each other in school, and here they were being asked to stand together and smile!

Farah's scowl deepened when she saw Umar sidle up to Sana.

Was he going to snatch the shoebox off her? That wasn't allowed. Sana clutched the box tightly in her lap.

Good. Sana was a bright girl. She wouldn't let Umar take the shoes. Would she?

Umar whispered something in Sana's ear.

Sana's mouth fell open and then she suddenly sprang to her feet, dropping the box to the floor. Umar reached down and removed the lid. Then he poked his fingers into the box and withdrew a huge spider.

Sana screamed as he waved the spider in front of her face.

"The shoes!" Naz called down. "Grab them!"

Umar either didn't hear her or chose to ignore her. He looked like he was having too good a time scaring Sana. The poor girl stood terrified on the spot.

"Now can we just have the bride and groom a little in front and the sisters by the side?" asked the photographer.

Farah ignored him. Turning on her heel, she rushed down the steps and grabbed the box off the floor.

"There are more in there!" Umar said, grinning mischievously.

"So, the spiders in the box were your top secret," Farah said.

"Yes," Umar nodded. "Just in case we had to scare you into giving the shoes back."

"I'm not scared of spiders!" Farah snapped.
She pulled the shoes out and then emptied the box
over Umar's head. Two more spiders fell out. It was
too much for Sana. Letting out a horrified scream, she
turned and fled.

"Why did you do that?" Umar exclaimed, dropping down to the floor. "Those spiders are my friends!".

"Umar!" Naz was beside them now. She had abandoned the family photographs too.

Umar was on the floor gently picking up his spiders. He produced a small glass from his pocket and placed them inside.

"I did what you told me to," he replied. "I scared that little girl."

"But you were supposed to grab the shoes!" Naz yelled with exasperation.

"You never said that!" Umar responded, looking quite cross.

Naz turned and stormed off.

Chapter 5
The cake

"Farah!" Anisa called from the stage. "We need to finish the photos. Get up here now."

Farah groaned. Not again! Her jaw had started to hurt before with all the smiling. Farah caught her mum's warning look from the stage and knew she had to go up. But first she'd have to hide the shoes.

"Rehan," Farah called the little boy over and whispered in his ear.

He nodded and took the box.

Farah made her way to the stage and stood stiffly next to her mum. Naz was already there with her family.

"I hope you've got my shoes," Sajid said to his sister.

"Of course I have," Naz responded.

"Phew!" Sajid jokingly wiped his forehead.

Farah strolled up to Naz.

"Oh, so you've got the shoes, have you? Or at least, that's what you want Sajid-bhai to think!"

"You haven't won yet," Naz hissed.

"Oh, but I think I have," Farah retorted. "It will only take me a minute to collect and present them to Sajid-bhai. Everyone will know that our side won. The bride's family has defeated the groom's."

Naz scowled as Farah returned to her place on the stage.

Click. Click. Click.

The photographs were never-ending. They carried on and on until Farah's mum put her hand up.

"I think that's enough," she said firmly. "It's time for dinner."

Sajid looked at Naz and then Farah.

"So, which of you has my shoes?" he asked. "I need to put them on so I can go down to the dinner table."

Farah smiled. "I have them," she said and walked off to collect the shoes.

The triplets were together again, hovering near the cake table.

Farah turned to find Naz had followed her and was standing close.

"Where are they?" Naz demanded.

"Do you really think I'm going to tell *you*?" Farah said, smirking.

Naz looked around. "The triplets don't have the box and yet they look very pleased with themselves."

"So?"

"That means the shoes are somewhere nearby," Naz guessed.

"It's over," Farah said. "You've lost and we've won."

Naz ignored her as her eyes travelled over the tables and the guests. "Where can they be ... hidden?"

Then she turned back towards the triplets. Rehan and Ahsan backed up against the cake table as if they were guarding it. Farah bit her lip. Honestly, why were those two making the hiding place so obvious?! Naz was going to guess the location if they carried on like this.

Farah was right. Naz worked it out and her face lit up.

"They're under the cake table, aren't they?"
Naz said aloud.

"No!" Farah denied.

Naz broke into a run and Farah followed.

Rehan and Ahsan, who were standing right in front of the table, saw the two enemies heading straight towards them.

"Ahh!" They shouted and jumped out of the way just in time.

Both girls dived under the table at the same time, but it was Naz whose hands covered the shoes. Farah wasn't going to give up so easily. She grabbed one shoe and pulled. Naz refused to let go. The scuffle intensified and both girls rose on their knees to secure a better grasp. Their heads banged on the table above, but they didn't notice because they were so consumed with holding onto the shoes.

"Give them to me now!" Naz screamed. "It's against the rules to snatch."

"You snatched them first!" Farah retorted.

"Let go!" Naz shouted. "We are the groom's side, and we always win!"

"This time the bride's family is going to win!" Farah shouted. "Let go!"

The table wobbled.

Farah and Naz continued to struggle over the shoes.

The table wobbled again, and a hush fell in the hall.

Sajid and Anisa stared in disbelief from their thrones. The guests gasped with a mixture of amusement and horror. The two sisters were taking this game more seriously than most players ever did.

Naz's mum shot up from her chair and hurried forward. So did Farah's mum. But they were too late. Before they could command their daughters to come out from beneath the tablecloth, the table gave one more wobble and then ...

SPLAT!

The three-tiered cake tumbled to the floor, breaking up into pieces to lie in a big mess of vanilla sponge and cream icing.

"Farah!" Her mum shouted.

"Come out at once!" Naz's mum commanded.

The two girls froze under the table. Their eyes met in horror as they realised what had happened. A second later, both dropped the shoes as if they were laced with poison. They crawled out with their heads bent and their outfits creased. When they finally raised their eyes, they wished they had remained hidden beneath the cloth. Their mums looked like they were going to explode with rage.

"How could you embarrass me like this?" Naz's mum hissed.

"At your own sister's wedding," Farah's mum spat out.

Sajid and Anisa had joined them by the cake table.

"I can't believe you two ruined my wedding cake," Anisa said miserably.

"I'm really sorry," Farah muttered.

"Me too," Naz added.

"Where are my shoes?" Sajid asked.

Farah and Naz exchanged a look. Even now, whoever presented the shoes would be considered the winner. The same thought crossed both their minds. Was it worth one last attempt to come out on top?

"Don't even think about it," Anisa said, guessing their thoughts. Her eyes flashed with anger. "Where are the shoes?"

Chapter 6
She who wins

"Under the table," Farah said.

Sajid crouched down, avoided the cake and reached under the table. As he pulled his arm out, his socks slipped on the shiny floor and he fell forward right into the cake mess.

Horrified gasps filled the hall from the guests that had witnessed it. Anisa heaved up her heavy bridal skirt revealing her high heels. She took a step forward and as she did, the heel caught in the hem of her skirt and sent her tumbling ahead. She landed next to Sajid in the cakey mess.

Farah and Naz stared in absolute horror at the bride and groom. The couple looked at each other and then burst out laughing. At first it was just the pair of them, but soon the mums joined in, as did all the guests. The only two people who stood with straight faces were Farah and Naz.

Neither could understand what was so funny.

They had both failed at the shoe game and the cake was ruined. Not to mention that the bride and groom's outfits were covered in vanilla sponge and icing.

Other family members helped Sajid and Anisa to their feet and they both went to clean their clothes.

The laughter died down.

Farah's mum turned to her. "Find a bin bag and clean this mess up."

"And you can help her, Naz," added Naz's mum.

Farah and Naz began the clean-up mission and by the time they'd managed to scrape the last bit of cake off the floor, everyone else had finished eating.

"You two can eat now," Farah's mum said.

Farah and Naz sat down but neither could eat much.

They were both full of guilt for ruining the cake.

"Finish your plates," Anisa said as she passed them on her way to the stage. "You've wasted enough food already."

"I'm so sorry about the cake," Farah blurted out.

Anisa shrugged. "It happened. It shouldn't have but it did. Let's not waste any more time over spilt cake."

Sajid laughed loudly at his wife's terrible joke.

Naz eyed her brother. "No wonder you two wanted to get married."

"Er, I don't think you should be cheeky after what you did," Sajid said.

Naz looked down at her plate, the guilt returning. "Sorry."

Sajid and Anisa returned to sit on their thrones with their mums. It was now time for the jewellery ceremony. Naz's mum had two red velvet boxes in her hands. She opened the top one and revealed a beautiful gold necklace with emerald and ruby stones.

"This is our family heirloom," she said. "It has belonged in our family for over 100 years. My husband's mother gave it to me on my wedding day and I am giving it to you on your wedding day."

Anisa took the box. "Thank you."

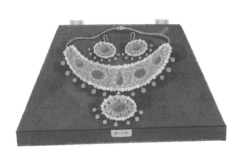

Naz's mum opened the second one. "This is the new set for you," she said. Farah knew this was the one Anisa had chosen herself at the jewellers.

"Sajid, place the necklace around Anisa's neck," Farah's mum instructed.

"One second," Sajid said. "We're missing the sisters. Farah, Naz, come up."

The two girls froze in their seats.

"Come on," Anisa called.

They walked up to the stage and stood next to their mums.

"Now that I've got my shoes back, I think I owe some money," Sajid said. "It seems there was no clear winner today, even though you both played the game with equal passion. So, I'm going to split the money between the both of you."

"I don't want it," Farah said. "I didn't win it fairly."

"Just take it," Anisa said. "Your new brother-in-law is giving you a gift."

"But before I hand over the money, I need you both to promise that you will stop this fighting," Sajid said. "We are family now after all."

Farah and Naz glanced at each other. They were indeed family now, but could they really become friends?

"Think of it as a wedding present to us,"
Anisa said. "It would make us happy to know our
sisters are getting on with each other."

Naz was the first to nod.

"Good girl," Sajid said and then turned to Farah.

"Oh, all right," she said.

"Now seal the end of the war between you with
a hug," Anisa instructed.

The two ex-enemies hugged awkwardly.

"See, that's better," Anisa said. "Anyway, what was the problem between you two?"

"Farah always seemed to hate me at school, so I tried to stay out of her way," Naz said.

"No, it was you who didn't like me," Farah said, looking surprised. "You never asked me to join your group when I moved to the school."

"All that hate over a little bit of confusion," Sajid said, shaking his head. "I'm glad that will stop now."

Farah turned to Naz. "Sorry you lost the game."

"You didn't exactly win either," Naz shot back.

For a second, they glared at each other and then burst out laughing.

It was true. Neither had won.

"Here you go," Sajid said, handing over the money. "I think you had accomplices too."

"Umar helped me," Naz said.

"The triplets were part of my team," Farah said.

The younger cousins were invited to the stage and were delighted to receive their share of the money.

"I'm glad your shoes didn't smell," Sana said. "I was worried all night that they would."

There was stunned silence and then Sajid said, "It's my wedding day and I had a good wash."

There was laughter all around.

The wedding photos

79

Old family wedding photos

wedding tent

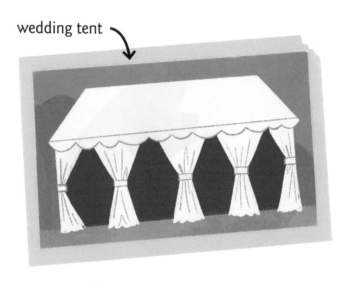

bride with face covered

hands washed
with water jug

traditional to eat
on the floor

Traditions

Women and girls on the bride's side
get together the day before
the wedding to dance and
decorate their hands with henna.
This is called mehndi.

The Nikaah is the marriage ceremony which is led
by an Imam.

A piece of paper has to be signed by the bride
and groom. It is called the Nikaah contract which is
evidence that a marriage has taken place.

The groom gives a gift of money to the bride, this
is called mahr. The bride's family never give money to
the groom.

Traditionally, the groom arrives on a horse (or a nice car if he prefers). Either way, he must make a grand entrance.

Having a wedding cake is a new tradition that has been added by South Asian Muslim families who live in Britain.

The groom's family hold a big feast the day after the wedding. This is called a walima.

In the Muslim tradition, the bride does not change her surname to the groom's surname. She keeps the name she was born with.

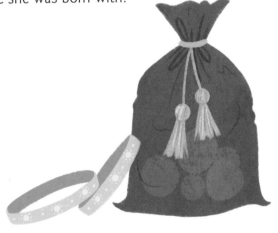

The wedding feast

South Asian Muslim weddings are big events where relatives, friends and neighbours are invited. It is quite normal to have at least 300 guests at a wedding and they all need to be fed!

Food plays a big part in a wedding. Whether a wedding has been enjoyed by the guests or not will depend on how good the food is.

The menu

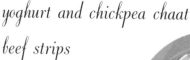

Starters:

meat samosa

meat kebabs

yoghurt and chickpea chaat

beef strips

fish cakes

chutney

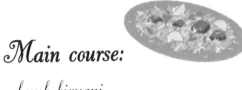

Main course:

lamb biryani

tandoori chicken

meat curry

naan

Dessert:

hot carrot halwa

with ice cream

Drinks:

water

fruit juice

fizzy drink

About the author

A bit about me ...

I am the author of over 20 children's books. Before my first book was published, I used to work in the Houses of Parliament, the Big Ben building.

Sufiya Ahmed

How did you get into writing?

I've written stories since I was eight years old. Reading was my favourite hobby, and my second favourite hobby was to write down everything that popped up in my imagination.

What do you hope readers will get out of the book?

I hope they will enjoy the battle for the shoes, and with it learn a little about South Asian Muslim wedding traditions.

Is there anything in this book that relates to your own experiences?

Yes, I've been a part of many games at family weddings to win the groom's shoes.

What is it like for you to write?

Writing is something I've always done. It's a bit like people who sing because they like to sing, or play football because they enjoy kicking a ball on a pitch. Writing is also important to me because I like to share ideas that are important to me.

What book did you love when you were young?

So many, how can I choose? My two favourite authors when I was very young were Enid Blyton and Roald Dahl. I borrowed all my books from the public library, and these were the ones available to me. I remember Dahl's *The Twits* was special.

Is anybody in the book based on someone you know in real life?

Ooh, that would be telling … I think I can say that the triplets are based on three very mischievous children I know. One of them is my nephew Rehan.

What would be your advice for children who have to go to a family wedding?

Enjoy it. Be respectful during the ceremony, throw your hands in the air when you're on the dance floor and eat to your heart's content. A wedding is a celebration.

Which of the characters in the story do you identify with the most, and why?

I've been on the bride's side and the groom's side at weddings and I can relate to Farah and Naz both. Trying to save the shoes, as well as trying to win them. All for good fun and to win money!

What is your favourite wedding tradition?

The battle for the groom's shoes.

About the illustrator

A bit about me …

I'm a Pakistani and Irish illustrator currently living in the UK. I love being on the beach on a sunny day, glitter and dancing around my kitchen while I cook. I also love bright colours, patterns and textures and like to use them throughout my work.

Abeeha Tariq

What made you want to be an illustrator?

Ever since I was young, I knew I wanted to draw. It's something that's always brought me a lot of calm and happiness – now I get to do it as a job! I love being able to bring characters and stories to life with illustration and each story is different and fun.

How did you get into illustration?

During 2020, I began to set myself little art challenges and really begin to practise and develop my own style. I posted my work on social media and became a part of the art and illustration community online and that was the beginning my professional illustration journey.

What did you like best about illustrating this book?

The characters are the key part of this story for me and I loved bringing to life all the fun and mischievous characters, like Farah, Naz and their cousins. I loved bringing the two families to life through colour and design.

What was the most difficult thing about illustrating this book?

Consistency! South Asian wedding outfits and jewellery have a lot of colour, detail and intricacies and I wanted to capture that in every illustration consistently — which was tricky at times!

Is there anything in this book that relates to your own experiences?

Absolutely — I have very special memories of going to family weddings with my own brother and cousins. It was always fun choosing colourful outfits, getting dressed up together, exploring the venue, dancing, and eating yummy food.

Have you ever been to a wedding like the one in the story?

Yes, I've been to a few family weddings where the bride and groom's side end up in (good-spirited) competition! It's all in good fun and we all get to enjoy some delicious biryani and dancing at the end of it all!

Book chat

What did you think of the book at the start? Did you change your mind at all as you read it?

Have you ever been to a big celebration like the one in this story? Would you like to?

If you could ask the author one question, what would it be?

If you had to pick one scene to act out, which would you choose? Why?

Does the book remind you of any other books you've read? How?

If you could talk to one character from the book, who would you pick? What would you say to them?

Which scene in this book stands out most for you? Why?

Do you think Farah and Naz will be friends now? Explain your answer.

Do you think Naz changed between the start and end of the story? If so, how?

Book challenge:

Ask around to hear some funny wedding stories or look at some wedding photo albums.

Collins
BIG CAT

Published by Collins
An imprint of HarperCollins*Publishers*

The News Building
1 London Bridge Street
London SE1 9GF
UK

Macken House
39/40 Mayor Street Upper
Dublin 1
D01 C9W8
Ireland

© HarperCollins*Publishers* Limited 2023

10 9 8 7 6 5 4 3 2

ISBN 978-0-00-862490-3

British Library Cataloguing-in-Publication Data
A catalogue record for this publication is available
from the British Library.

Download the teaching notes and
word cards to accompany this book at:
http://littlewandle.org.uk/signupfluency/

Get the latest Collins Big Cat news at
collins.co.uk/collinsbigcat

Author: Sufiya Ahmed
Illustrator: Abeeha Tariq (ASH Literary)
Publisher: Lizzie Catford
Product manager: Caroline Green
Series editor: Charlotte Raby
Commissioning editor: Suzannah Ditchburn
Development editor: Catherine Baker
Project manager: Emily Hooton
Content editor: Daniela Mora Chavarría
Copyeditor: Catherine Dakin
Proofreader: Gaynor Spry
Typesetter: 2Hoots Publishing Services Ltd
Cover designer: Sarah Finan
Production controller: Katharine Willard

Collins would like to thank the teachers and
children at the following schools who took part in
the trialling of Big Cat for Little Wandle Fluency:
Burley And Woodhead Church of England Primary
School; Chesterton Primary School; Lady Margaret
Primary School; Little Sutton Primary School;
Parsloes Primary School.

Printed and bound in the UK by Page Bros Group Ltd

MIX
Paper | Supporting
responsible forestry
FSC
www.fsc.org
FSC™ C007454

This book is produced from independently
certified FSC™ paper to ensure
responsible forest management.

For more information visit:
www.harpercollins.co.uk/green